INNER MANN

by

Steven Dearden and Ken Hassell

Children on a farm were expected to help with a wide range of jobs including watering the horses and cattle, cutting thistles and picking stones. At hay time the children helped to drag the ricks of hay from the fields and – especially in wet weather – to stook the corn, often working into the night in an emergency.

FURTHER READING

Briggs, H., *A Harvest of Memories*, 2002
Cashin, T. L., *A Michael Village Trail*, 3rd edition, 1979
Kermode, George, *Laxey, As I Remember It*, 1993
Kneen, Norman (ed.), *Marown Parish*, 1986
Kniveton, Gordon N., *The Onchan Story*, 1992
Lewthwaite, Priscilla, *History of Union Mills*, 1986
Quilliam, John, *Gems from 'Know Your Parish'*, 3 vols., 1979–81
Radcliffe, W. & C., *A History of Kirk Maughold*, 1979
Radcliffe, W. & C., *Kirk Bride: A Miscellany*, 1982
Rimington, John, *Features and History of the Meayll Peninsula*, 2000
Vale, Denis, *On Foot in Patrick*, 2000
Vernon, Juan, *A Sulby History Trail*, 1999

New Road, Laxey during the 'Big Snow' of February 1895, in which snow fell relentlessly for 33 hours. It was the severest blizzard on record and drifts lay thick on the ground for many weeks. Away from the towns, country lanes were covered to the tops of the hedges and low-lying cottages were completely buried. Shops and a bakery, until recent years the village co-op, were later built on the left of New Road by Robert Williamson, whose newspaper shop is on the right in this view. This is now used by Laxey Village Commissioners, with Williamson's former office serving as their boardroom. Down some steps behind the building was an acetylene gas plant which provided heating for the office and shop. Part of the ground floor housed Williamson's famous mineral water works from where 'pop' was supplied all over the Island.

INTRODUCTION

In this, our eighth book of old photographs of the Isle of Man, we look at 'Inner Mann', the rural areas away from the six main towns and resorts of the Island. Regrettably, space does not permit inclusion of a completely comprehensive selection of pictures, but we have endeavoured to illustrate the character of these rural parts of the Island. The photographs are arranged alphabetically by parish, and the 'Kirk' that historically belongs before the names of all but Ballaugh and Jurby has been omitted for this purpose.

The years covered – the 1860s to the 1940s – were ones of dramatic change in the Isle of Man, and the areas illustrated continue to change today. The stables that once housed farm horses have fallen into ruin, cottagers no longer keep their own pig, and traction engines have long since ceased to be a feature of the harvest field. Fortunately much that is admirable still remains, however, and the Manx countryside has been spared the worst excesses of the factory farmer, if not always those of the speculative developer.

The growth of the holiday trade was the Island's great economic success story between 1863 and 1914 and the countryside shared in the benefits that sprang from this. Manx farmers profited from the fact that goods were comparatively expensive to import, and the strength of the tourist industry meant that the greater part of their output could be sold locally. The dependence on tourism was emphasised by the decline of other industries. Laxey, the last of the Island's mines, closed in 1929 and as early as 1914 only 57 fishing vessels were operational. The big drawback to the tourist industry was that it only operated for four months of the year, leaving many unemployed during the winter.

The First World War saw a temporary increase in the acreage of land under crops on the Isle of Man, boosted not least by the needs of the vast internment camp at Knockaloe. The growing of grain crops soon became unprofitable after the war though and by 1939 there had been a decrease of 25% in the amount of arable land. Large swathes were taken out of cultivation and many marginal hill farms abandoned, although the number of sheep and acreage of permanent grassland markedly increased.

Profitable farming was achieved by comparatively few and while the effects of the Depression were demoralising for the farmer, conditions were certainly poorer for farm labourers. Servants and labourers still had to gather at the hiring fair at Hollantide (12 November) to seek the security of regular employment for the following twelve months. Working hours were from 6 a.m. to 6 p.m. Monday to Saturday and men were expected to work Sunday mornings with only one Sunday afternoon off in two. Farmers even resisted the introduction of the recommended early 4 p.m. finish on Saturdays. The picturesque thatched cottages were in reality all too often crowded, dark and damp. Labourers' wives lit their homes with candles or paraffin lamps, carried heavy buckets of water from the well and cooked over a coal fire. With virtually no labour-saving devices almost every waking minute was spent feeding, washing and clothing the family, with little time or energy left for other interests.

The increased movement between town and village illustrated to country-dwellers that such drudgery did not have to be endured, and many left for the town. Wages fell immediately after 1918 but those who stayed were gradually able to demand and achieve a higher income and standard of living. Greater mobility came with the development of the rural bus service – which was introduced in 1927 when two different companies began to compete for business – and as the twentieth century progressed children benefited from a better education than that which had been available to their parents.

Generally though there was little incentive to mechanise or take risks and the growing importance of the tractor and decline in horse husbandry only really gathered pace in the 1940s. Horses were relatively cheap, early tractors were unreliable and badly designed and combine harvesters found it difficult to cope with the small and awkward field shapes of Manx farms. In 1939 the number of tractors on the Island was only 114 and although this figure had increased to 621 by 1948 there were still only four combine harvesters. The demise of the traction engine came about more as a result of the high price and shortage of coal following the war than out of a desire to modernise.

As late as the 1950s the appearance of the Manx countryside differed little from that of Victorian times. The thatched cottages and quaint farms had become objects to be admired and photographed, and despite the problems of those who lived there, the countryside attracted an increasing number of tourists, as well as retired persons and commuters who chose to live there permanently. We hope you enjoy these glimpses of a way of life that has changed dramatically but still not quite been lost.

Andreas is a parish of narrow winding lanes, whitewashed cottages, fertile land and large farmhouses surrounded by groves of trees. Its population is scattered and the village of Kirk Andreas forms a focal point in the north of the Island. The only place to keep up its village club and club day procession, every year on Ascension Day the men and boys of Kirk Andreas attend church and parade round the village wearing their blue and white club sashes. T. H. Midwood published this postcard of the village which was posted on 21 March 1907. The view looks towards the school, while on the left is the sender's home, Auburn House, one of the most handsome dwellings in the village with its combination of Sulby stone and Ballacorey brick partly concealed by ivy.

ANDREAS . I.O.M

Church control of education gave way to that of the School Committee in 1875 and the old Parochial School was replaced by this new building at the beginning of the twentieth century. 44 infants and 80 older pupils were accommodated, the facilities an advance on many smaller village schools where one teacher often had to teach children of all ages in one class. The only licensed establishment in the whole of Andreas is the Grosvenor Hotel. 31 of its 38 inns were closed in the 1830s by the Rector of Andreas, Benjamin Philpot and the Captain of the Parish, John Kneale, who refused to renew existing licences. During the Second World War Kirk Andreas benefited from the presence of the nearby Air Gunnery School. The Clegg family's shop in the village was open from 7 a.m. until midnight during this period selling countless sandwiches at twopence and cups of tea for a penny. Mr Clegg did a roaring trade in Raleigh bicycles which he sold to the airmen at 90 shillings each, or £1 down and two shillings and sixpence a month to pay.

Kentraugh House and its estate was a typical English gentleman's residence of a type rarely seen on the Isle of Man. Its owners, the Gawne family, were the most important landowners in the south of the Island. The high walls surrounding the estate have two tall arches in them, one of which carries a plaque inscribed 'Judge not your fellow man's condition until you be in his position'. Kentraugh has extensive gardens, although originally more interest was shown in forestry than ornamental gardening. The basic plan of the garden is fairly typical of larger Manx country houses, with twin drives enclosing an area of parkland. Kentraugh was noted for the quality of its hothouse-raised fruit crops, and also had its own farm as well as a slaughterhouse and an ice house. At the peak of its prosperity, 50 staff were employed on the estate. The Primitive Methodists used to hold camp meetings in the open air on the claddaghs (river meadows) at Kentraugh. The Colby River has been put to many uses here including the powering of a private mill within the grounds to provide for the needs of the estate. The Gawnes also operated a bone mill, used to grind bones for fertiliser.

BALLAUGH, I.O.M

To 'Go to Ballaugh' was once a commonly-used Manx phrase meaning to withdraw from everyday life and worldly activity. The parish had once been prosperous, however, with over 100 men involved in the seasonal fishing, three blacksmiths, three breweries, two nail-makers' forges, and even a small hat factory. In 1840 the population stood at 1,500, three times the figure in 1900 when this photograph was taken. The 'modern' village of Ballaugh grew around the main Ramsey to Peel road and centred on the humpback bridge made famous by the TT races. When the first race was held in 1904, the narrow roads with their varying surfaces, high hedges and wandering farm animals made the hour-long lap of the course a trying experience. Ballaugh is a part of the Island that has suffered less than most from the ravages of the modern developer.

Ballaugh police station shown on an Alfred Moore postcard of 1906. The late 1870s saw the rural constable for the area replaced by a permanent sergeant, one James Cubbon. Soon after this postcard was produced, however, the station was closed and moved to Kirk Michael as part of the changes recommended by a 1904 review of the Island's force.

Ballaugh's Railway Hotel was formerly known as the North Star and is mentioned as such in George Wood's account of the Island in 1811. The name was changed when the Manx Northern Railway opened in 1879; the then landlord Richard Hughes realised that he was on to a good thing as the railway dramatically increased passing traffic from locals and visitors.

The walk to Kirk Braddan was one of the most popular in the neighbourhood of Douglas. Having passed through the grounds of the Nunnery and crossed Pulrose meadows, the Saddle Road was reached. This skirted the grounds of Kirby – an ancient estate on which a mansion house had been built by 1405 – before winding down to Kirk Braddan Church. This picture shows the Deemster's Cottages on the Saddle Road, which from the mid-nineteenth century were let to employees of Sir William Drinkwater, Southern Deemster (his uncle, Sir George Drinkwater, had acquired the Kirby estate in 1840). Saddle Road was named after a saddle-shaped stone projecting from a nearby wall. According to one story this saddle was used by the fairies; another tale said that if you sat on the stone and made a wish it would come true. 'Deemster' is the term used for a judge on the Isle of Man.

The normal tranquillity of Braddan Bridge has been broken by the three-lap 1923 sidecar TT race. The nearest machine is that of leader H. Langman, while in the distance the eventual winner, Freddie Dixon, can be seen. He remains the only rider to have won both a sidecar and solo TT race on the Mountain Circuit. More permanent racing facilities could be found in Braddan at the Belle Vue racecourse, which opened in 1912 after conversion from a sports stadium. The old racecourse at the Strang near Douglas was still operating at the time, but facilities there were poor. Belle Vue proved very popular but fell foul of the Betting & Gaming Act and had to close in 1931. Douglas Town Council bought the property and it eventually became the King George V Park, before being transformed into the National Sports Centre.

At the point where the old and new Castletown roads met, a sharp descent led into the small village of Kewaigue, where W. Comery took this photograph of some interesting old farm buildings. Note the dovecotes attached to the wall of the building. Sometimes these would be set directly into the wall, the pigeons providing a welcome source of fresh meat in wintertime as well as a source of valuable manure. However, the damage they did to crops had to be taken into account, and pigeons would rarely be kept on a farm today. A hare or rabbit can be made out in the hutch on the left – probably another source of food – and there is a millstone resting against the barn wall.

The secret of a good potato crop is to plant a variety well-suited to an area's particular soil, and if necessary to enhance this with appropriate fertiliser. Mr Titterton's potato experiment with sulphate of potash seems to have paid dividends for him. This promotional card was produced in association with the Irish Board of Agriculture and information on the reverse stresses the value of adding potash to manure to promote maximum yield from a variety of crops, including potatoes. On the Isle of Man the potato crop would be dug up with a 'grep' and collected in baskets. The main crop was then put into clamps or long butts and covered with soil and straw for sorting and bagging later in the winter, while the small potatoes would usually be fed to pigs or cattle or used for seed.

Potato experiment by Mr. G. TITTERTON, Quines Hill, Port Soderick, I.O.M. Rich Chalk, Heavy Soil.

GAIN from 1 cwt. Sulphate of Potash – 1 ton 15 cwt. Potatoes.

Situated just two miles from Douglas, Union Mills was originally known as the Doway, the change of name taking place after the construction of a second mill there in 1807. This manufactured woollen products and was situated alongside the old corn mill. The village received a second boost to its development in 1873 when the opening of the railway line from Douglas to Peel made it the centre of the local farming community. Rather surprisingly, the village stores in Union Mills (now the Central Stores) are advertising Ariel motorcycles and cycles in this view from the very early 1900s (alongside more typical adverts for Fry's cocoa and Lyons tea). On the left and still standing today are the Union Mills themselves, closed by this date and soon to find new use as the premises of Cowen's laundry, dyers and cleaners, the forerunner of Clucas's laundry.

Now demolished, the Cronk was a small farm near Union Mills. This idyllic scene on the Cronk road is reproduced from a post-war Isle of Man Publicity Board photograph, captioned on the reverse: 'A delightful rural scene in the Isle of Man. The Isle of Man has been aptly called "The photographer's paradise".'

A 1930s photograph of Bride taken from beside the churchyard wall. The church, rectory and half a dozen cottages originally constituted the whole of the village. Unlike in England, the presence of a parish church rarely concentrated the population into a cluster around it. The Manx system was one of small landowners, scattered homesteads and many small chapels or keeills. Gradually the village developed, however, and Bride's post office opened in 1869, having originally been located at the house of Richard Pass, the schoolmaster. Letters arrived from Ramsey at 8.40 a.m. and recipients had only until 11 a.m. – when the mail was collected – to compose their replies. St Bridget's was built in 1872 with masonry from the old church used to provide foundations for the new building. The old churchyard contained several Norse crosses which are now safely kept inside the church. One gravestone of particular interest is that of John Cowell who lost part of his arm at the Battle of Trafalgar and became known as 'Hook' Cowell thereafter.

ON THE ROAD TO GLEN HELEN

The thatched cottages at Ballig Bridge feature in an increasingly derelict condition in many photographs of the TT races but are still in good condition in this early postcard view. The task of thatching and repairing the thatch involved the whole family and the help of neighbours. The roof work was done by the men while the women did the preparatory work, pulling the thatch into smooth 'welts' for laying on the 'scraas' (thin sods of earth which were placed on laths on the roof before the thatch was laid) in thick, even pads.

BALLAMOAR

This 1907 postcard of Ballamoar Castle shows the brand new gothic-style mansion which had been completed only three years earlier. It stands on the site of a much older building which for centuries had been home to a branch of the Christian family. Kelly Bros. built the new house for Alfred Curphey, who had great plans to drain the Curraghs but departed from the Island in a hurry, leaving a trail of debts behind. In 1908 it was sold to Baron Francis Rom, a wealthy Belgian manufacturer, and it is to Brussels that this postcard was posted. The occupant of the old house, William Farrant, had planted numerous rare plants and trees and Ballamoar's park and gardens were famous for the number and variety of species they contained. Jurby is a small and sparsely populated parish, sandy and dry to the north and wet and marshy to the southern, Curraghs side.

THE BRIDGE. GLEN AULDYN.

There were several cottages and small farmhouses in the lower part of Glen Auldyn together with a corn and flour mill and a woollen manufactory. Although larger than the Dhoon or Ballaglass Glen, it is only towards the head of Glen Auldyn that the scenery becomes as impressive. The bridge at the top of the lower glen is shown here with the small chapel visible to the left.

GLEN AULDYN.
AFTER THE STORM.

At the entrance to Glen Auldyn is Milntown, the scene of the most famous battle in Manx history, where in 1079 Godred Crovan defeated the Manx at Skyhill. It is also the seat of the Christian family, once the most powerful on the Island. They controlled not only the mill here, by the Crossag path, but also water mills in Lezayre, Maughold and Jurby. The 'falls' are an attractive feature of the lower glen, which is seen here after the storm of 18 September 1930. During this all the footbridges in the glen were swept away and trees were wedged under the railway bridge, moving it several inches out of line so that trains could not run into Ramsey for some days. Two landslides higher up the glen added to the problems.

The Ginger Hall Hotel at Sulby replaced an earlier building destroyed by fire in 1888. The landlord at the time had been refused a renewal of his licence and it was noted that he did not seem to be making much of an effort to put the fire out! The Scottish Tavern (as it had been known) dated from the 1790s and it is thought the name of the new hotel came from the locally-famous ginger beer that was brewed on the premises. The sign for Hovis bread was typical of those found outside many country inns and cafes on the Island between the wars.

A gap between some buildings in Sulby marks a public watering place where cattle could be brought to the Sulby River to drink. The rick in the background shows that thatching was not confined to cottages and farm buildings but also used for haystacks. Most farm labourers would have been efficient thatchers and miniature thatched stacks were made for Harvest Festival displays, with interlaced Celtic designs worked into them. Situated nearby, Sulby Bridge had been improved on several occasions and was unusually wide and much longer than it needed to be for the size of the river at this point. A gap in the parapet leading to some steps gave access to the river for householders to fetch water, a facility later used regularly to replenish passing traction engines.

The Sulby Glen Hotel was built before 1800 to provide accommodation for fishing parties from Ramsey and Douglas. The building has been extended over the years with two bays added to the Ramsey side and the incorporation of Dr Anderson's house (the white building) to the west. A popular bowling green was situated to the rear, as was a small village bakehouse. This pre-1900 photograph has been taken from what later became the site of Caley's shop. The hotel's stables can be seen beyond Dr Anderson's house.

The construction of a branch line of the Snaefell Mountain Tramway from the Bungalow Hotel (built in 1895 halfway up Snaefell) to Tholt-y-Will had been seriously considered in 1896 but came to nothing. The link was made in 1907, however, when a motor bus service (the first on the Island) was introduced using two Argus sixteen-seat charabancs. The tearooms and hotel at Tholt-y-Will, illustrated here, were the key attraction, providing quite elaborate meals as part of the full day tours on offer. A notice adjacent to the tearooms read: 'Weather and other circumstances permitting (Sundays excepted) the time of departure of the last motor charabanc from Tholt-y-Will to the Bungalow is 5.45 p.m., to connect with the last Electric Car from Snaefell Summit to Laxey'. Popular right up to 1939, trips to Tholt-y-Will were revived in the 1950s when a round trip from Douglas was introduced using a variety of modes of transport: electric tram between Douglas and Laxey; mountain tramway from Laxey to the Bungalow; motor bus via Tholt-y-Will to Sulby Glen; steam train from Sulby Glen to Ramsey; and finally electric tram back to Douglas. Few took advantage of the attractive offer, however, and trips ceased in 1958 when the popular Bungalow Hotel was demolished.

The Laxey Wheel was a major visitor attraction, and on arriving at Dumbell's Terrace, the road up to it, a whole range of amusements was on offer to tempt tourists. Edward Killip ran many of the sideshows including coconut shies and football skittles. The primary role of the wheel was, however, an industrial one and lower down the valley was the washing floor of the lead and silver mines (illustrated here), now the site of Valley Gardens. Here the mined ore was raked onto revolving tables to be washed and hand sorted. It was then passed into jaw crushers powered by this waterwheel fed by a race from the river. The elaborate machinery needed to perform the washing and sorting remained largely unchanged following its construction in 1848 until the closure of the mines in 1929. On the other side of the main Ramsey to Douglas road the huge 'deads' of waste material can be seen.

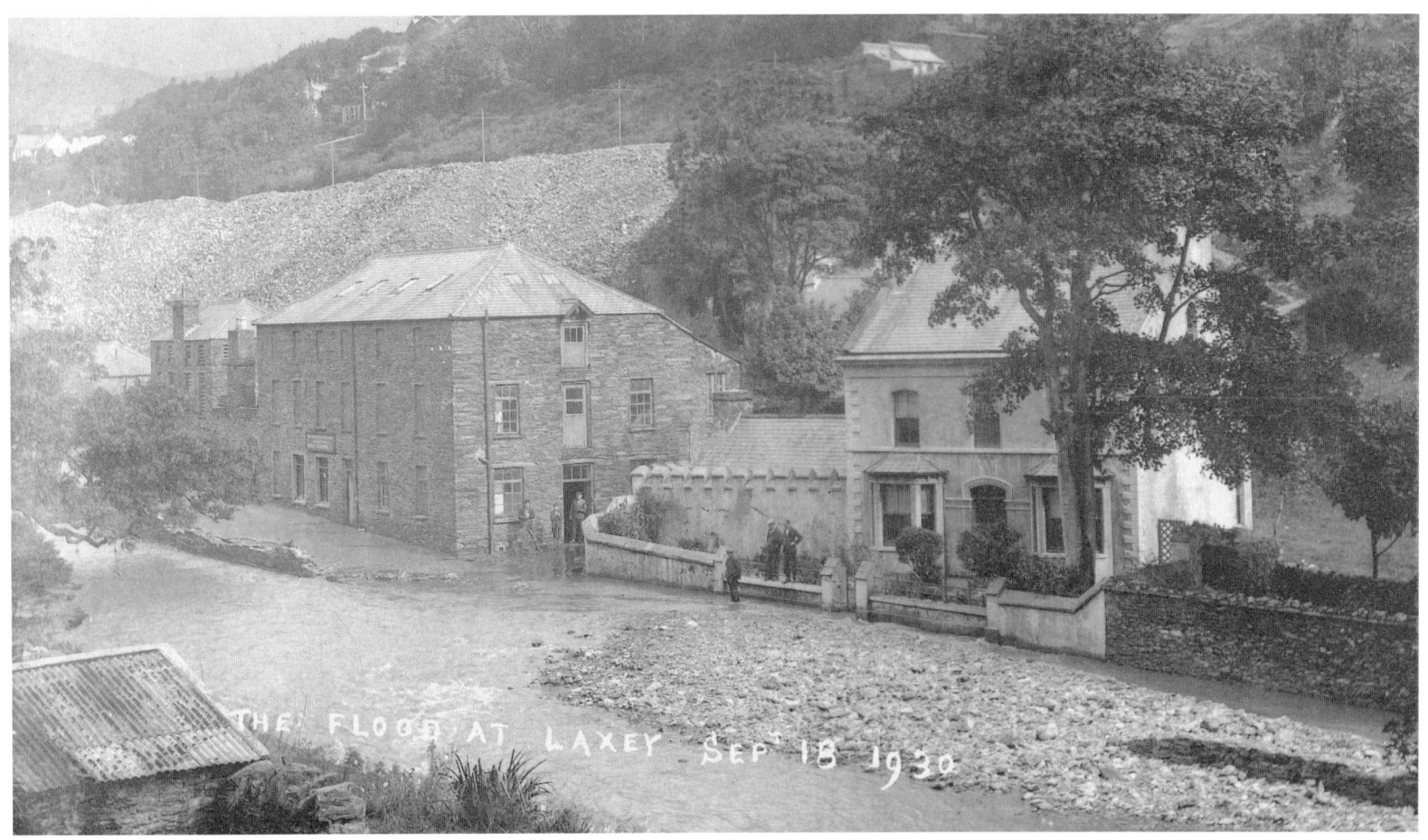

Commencing at 8 p.m. on 17 September 1930 and continuing until four o'clock the next morning, a terrible rainstorm caused widespread damage across the Isle of Man, with over four inches of rain falling in Ramsey alone. The 'Great Storm', as it became known, affected Laxey particularly badly as the river burst its banks there, swept bridges away and deposited over 4,000 tons of rubble in its wake. Most of the district was left without electricity, water or sewerage. The destruction prompted a visit by the Lieutenant Governor who launched a distress fund. Flooding damage at the St George's Woollen Mills is illustrated in this picture, which also shows mounds of mine 'deads' in the background. Still operating today, the mills were established in 1881 by Egbert Rydings, a retired Lancashire silk-weaver and follower of John Ruskin's ideas of craft workers organised in a workers' co-operative. The building dates from 1850 and was built as a corn mill known as Moughtin's Mill.

A 1930s view of Garwick village looking down the hill to Garwick Mill. From the turn of the century until about 1922 the miller was John James Faragher, whose brother ran the Golden Meadow Mill at Castletown. When he gave up the mill at Garwick he opened a coal merchant's business in Laxey. The whitewashed stone mill building survives as a private residence with its wheel in a fairly good state of preservation.

The Cloven Stones can still be seen today, but are now in the garden of a bungalow near the old entrance to Garwick Glen. Before their enclosure, in the days of horse-drawn wagonettes, drivers would stop at the stones and tell their passengers about how they clapped together whenever the Kirk Lonan church bell was heard. Much of the ancient cairn has been destroyed but it is said to mark the resting place of an invading Welsh prince.

TEDDY BEAR AND KEEPER AT GROUDLE GLEN

WALTON

Groudle Glen sits on the boundary between the parishes of Lonan and Onchan, and by 1900 over 100,000 visitors annually were using the scenic miniature railway within the glen. There were cafes on the cliff top and headland overlooking Port Groudle, and a hotel at the head of the glen. The zoo at Groudle Glen was famous for its sea lions and polar bears but brown bear cubs were an added attraction for a period prior to 1914. They may have been well looked after but it is unclear what happened to them when they became fully grown. Hopefully they were returned to the Belle Vue Zoo in Manchester where they were born. Certainly Jumbo, one of the polar bears, made that journey, but unfortunately only as a stuffed exhibit after his death. Live music, open-air dance floors and electric lighting throughout the glen added to its natural attractions.

Ballasalla was once the largest village on the Island, built more to the English pattern than the usual low-density scattered habitations of a typical Manx village, perhaps due to the strong influence exerted by the nearby Rushen Abbey. Silverdale lies half a mile from Ballasalla in Malew Parish and is best approached from Rushen Abbey along the banks of the Silverburn River. Long a favourite destination for Sunday school parties, Silverdale Glen is famous for its boating lake and water-powered carousel. The lake was formed by the dam created for Silverdale corn mill and all the attractions were run by the Quine family, owners of the mill.

Taking the Crossag road from Ballasalla and up Black Hill leads to the Orrisdale road junction. This undated photograph shows Robert Radcliffe at Harry Moor's Mill, Black Hill, with a threshing machine and a group of well-dressed boys who look too young to be farm workers. Some haystacks had a rectangular base, others the traditional Manx circular base. These were called thurrans and traditionally contained the number of sheaves that could be dealt with in one threshing with the old flails. A flail was a simple wooden device consisting of a wooden bar with a hinged handle, which was used to strike a sheaf of wheat near the grain end, thereby separating the grain from the straw. Flailing was often done indoors on wet days, with a piece of canvas placed on the ground to collect the grain.

Today the overriding impression of Derbyhaven is one of tranquillity. The hotel, so popular in the early years of Ronaldsway Aerodrome, has gone, as has the small fleet of pleasure boats, and traffic is now largely bound for Castletown Golf Course and the beauties of Langness. Derbyhaven was however the principal port for the south of the Island right through the rule of the Norse kings and the Derbys and into the nineteenth century. Early guidebooks warned that the road round the head of Derbyhaven to St Michael's Isle was not passable to carriages because of the heavy influxes of sand from the dunes there, although the building of properties along the road during the nineteenth century put an end to the problem. A magnifying glass reveals two chickens pecking about in the road in this view.

When this photograph was taken in 1913 the *Christino Cruz* was a newly-built riverboat destined for use in the shallow waters of South America. After leaving Preston on 11 February, she quickly found that her engines and steering were useless in heavy seas and disaster was only just avoided on several occasions before she grounded between Hango Hill and Derbyhaven. The vessel attracted many local sightseers before she was refloated using greased poles and taken to Castletown for repair and return to Lytham St Annes.

A milk float from Creggans Farm posed outside the premises of J. Swales, photographer, in Castletown. The floats were three sided with a detachable backboard and a slatted floor to allow rain or spilt milk to run off. Other than the kegs of milk, the only item on the float would be the driver's detachable box seat which contained the measures. Great pride was taken in their appearance and milk floats usually had painted scrollwork with the farm name on the frontboard. Creggans Farm was at Ronaldsway and its land was incorporated into the airport.

The Village Store   CROSBY. I.O.M.

Motorised traffic was still almost unknown when local photographer David Collister took this picture of the main Douglas to Peel road through Crosby c.1905 showing the village store on the right. Tourism had become important to Crosby following the arrival in 1873 of the railway, and the village bustled with visitors during the season. A wide range of goods was stocked at the shop including candles, flour, carbolic soap, bundles of firewood, lengths of cloth, and paraffin, which was kept safely outside away from the thatched roof. Although Douglas is only about three miles from Crosby, a trip there would still have been a rare treat for its villagers.

CROSBY WESLEYAN CHURCH AND SCHOOL I.O.M.

The Revd Robert Aitken was an eccentric character best known for developing the bizarre Eyreton Castle in the 1830s. The name came from his wife's family, Eyres, the source of his wealth, and was applied to other local properties including Eyreton Terrace in Crosby. Having rarely been on good terms with Bishop Murray, Aitken lost his post at St George's Church in Douglas and it was after this that he turned his attention to the building of the castle, which was intended to be a religious college. After a warning he believed came from God, Aitken entered a period of sixteen days of continuous fasting and prayer at the end of which he built a chapel (left) for the Methodists of Crosby. Although still a Church of England minister, he then started to preach at Methodist chapels all over the Island. He could have a near-hypnotic effect on those who heard him, although his relations with the authorities were never without controversy. The separate Sunday school building (right) was opened in 1904, an unusually grand structure for the Island's Methodists.

Many pigs were kept in the fields skirting the Island's towns and Ramsey was no exception. They were sometimes to be found in the towns themselves and on one famous occasion Thomas Keig, the photographer and first mayor of Douglas, lost a lot of votes in an election by advocating that pigs should not be allowed within the area surrounding dwelling houses. A pig was driven around Douglas in a cart, much to the amusement of his opponents. These fine specimens appear on a postcard with a Ramsey postmark.

This fascinating Samuel Rothwell photograph dates from the 1860s and shows the Maughold parish cross in its original location by the churchyard gate. These parish or market crosses used to stand outside every parish church, and it was from here that sumners would make public announcements (a sumner was a minor court official who executed decrees and judgements for the ecclesiastical courts). Maughold churchyard is thought to be the largest in Britain and the cross bears the second oldest depiction of the three legs of Mann, only that on the Manx sword of state being older. Prior to the opening of the cross house at Maughold in 1906, the Scandinavian monuments were scattered about the churchyard and village green.

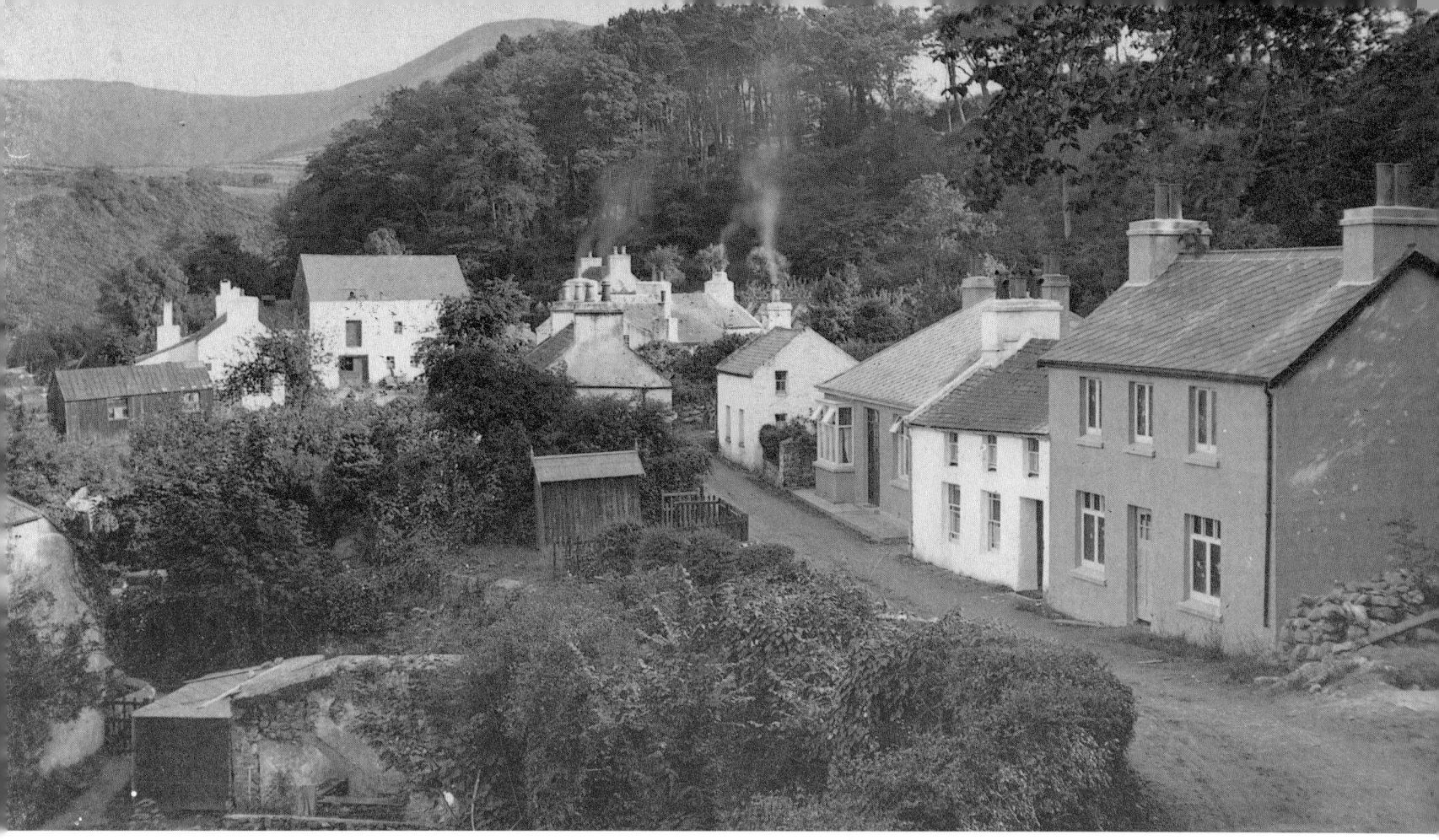

Glen Wyllin village was home to four mills powered by its small stream. As well as corn and flour mills it also supported a brewery from 1820–60, the house connected with this later becoming the village school. Despite its relative prosperity, however, Glen Wyllin was almost completely cut off from nearby Kirk Michael village. Access to Glen Wyllin was difficult at any time and almost impossible in winter, the poor roads and steep descents being unsuitable for wheeled vehicles. The construction of a bridge over the Glen Wyllin stream in 1831 improved matters and the arrival of the Manx Northern Railway in 1879 opened up new opportunities for the village's inhabitants, enabling them to work further from home, send produce to market or simply shop in Douglas or Peel. Access was also much easier for visitors and the railway brought particularly great changes to the portion of the glen seaward of the Peel road.

This George Cowen postcard shows Station Road, Kirk Michael in 1906. The opening of the railway in 1879 brought important changes to the village, not least the development of Michael's small-scale tourist industry. All the properties in Station Road were built in the years following the railway's arrival and nearly everyone would have taken in visitors at this time. Kirk Michael's church was completed in 1835 and could seat 650 people, with a pew allowed for each quarterland. (A quarterland consisted of a quarter of a 'treen', an area of land comprising 200–400 acres. Quarterlands were formerly quite important administrative divisions used for fixing land taxes.) Situated a little to the west of the old church, it was built on part of the vicar's glebe. A story from the time of the Big Snow of 1895 relates how a clergyman walked along a snow drift to the top of the church and sat on the roof!

UNHE CROSS KIRK MICHAEL

The parish's collection of ancient cross slabs is now kept in the north transept of Kirk Michael church. This early postcard shows the giant Joalf's Cross in its original position outside the church gates with the old school behind it. At eleven feet tall, with the top 6½ feet decorated, it is the largest cross on the Island. It was dug up in the eighteenth century, half a mile to the north in the side of Cronk-y-Chrogher, a hill named from a gallows formerly sited there. In the early years of the twentieth century the narrowest portion of the road though Kirk Michael made it difficult for even two horse-drawn vehicles to pass. With the increase in motor traffic, it was inevitable by the 1930s that the road would have to be widened and many properties were demolished to permit this.

The old village of Onchan, known as Kiondroghad until at least the 1830s, consisted of a few cottages, only one of which still survives. These were concentrated round the Butt or Church Road on the old packhorse route from Douglas to Ramsey, which crossed the bridge here before continuing up the Groudle Back Road. This part of the village still remains unspoiled despite the disconcerting expansion of much of the area since the war.

Now called Welch House, the small ecclesiastical-looking building at the bottom of the Butt was actually the old Onchan Infant School. This was built in 1842 to accommodate the overspill from the Parish School situated on the opposite side of the road. Conditions in the old school were damp and unhealthy, but despite this it was 1876 before further school accommodation was built and it was closed. The eccentric Revd John Howard, violently opposed to state education, did everything in his power to delay the building of the new school. Welch House is named after John Welch who designed the nearby St Peter's Church in the same style in 1830. Local labour was employed wherever possible, and the family of one of the builders, John Skillicom, is still involved in the trade. St Peter's opened in 1833 and a new vicarage followed in 1842, the same year as the infant school.

In the nineteenth century the Cadman family, owners of Howstrake, one of the Island's biggest and most productive farms, also farmed Ballachrink and Ballachurry. Now the buildings have been demolished and all but a small portion of the three farms has been built on, victims of Onchan's urban sprawl. The village joiners who made vehicles such as this one, photographed at Ballachrink Farm, were highly skilled men and the many examples of their craft that have survived to the present day are testimony to their abilities.

Returning towards Douglas via the West Baldwin Valley would take one past Ballig Farm. A tiny hamlet with a Methodist chapel and a clubroom, Ballig was the site of an important watermill. Here the farmer and his wife (identified only as Fred and Elsie) are pictured in front of the stone farmhouse.

Abbeylands is one of the last few real farming communities left on the Island. As work for blacksmiths declined with the introduction of tractors, the smithy at Abbeylands became the only survivor of this trade in the whole parish. Situated just above Sir George's Bridge, it was run by Ted Leece who later worked from a shed at the entrance to Abbeylands Young Men's Club. Abbeylands post office operated from 1898 until 1941 and was continuously run by members of the Leece family. Agnes Leece was postmistress at the time of its closure. Sir George's Bridge, named after Sir George Drinkwater, a contributor to its construction, was rebuilt in 1984. Farms and houses in Abbeylands were leased from the Abbey of Rushen and until comparatively recently tithes were still payable to the church.

Retracing the route back from Ballachrink, a branch road ascends a steep hill and, passing the old vicarage, the higher land of Ballamodha is reached before St Luke's Church comes into view. There were several farms in the area, all farmed by Kellys who became known by the name of their farm. These included Kelly Ballacoyne and Kelly Ballamodha, both still farmed by a Philip Kelly today. A farmyard scene such as this one at Ballamodha – once a common sight – is all too rarely seen today.

FOXDALE. I.O.M.

KEE. PHOTO. IV

This general view of Foxdale shows the village *c.*1905, at the end of its period as one of the major mining centres on the Island. During its 80 years of operation, the Isle of Man Mining Company regularly produced over 1,000 tons of lead annually at Foxdale. The peak year for silver production at Foxdale was 1896 when 188,473 ounces were mined; a more typical annual figure for the years 1862–1900 was 50–70,000 ounces.

The view south from the Niarbyl shows the only part of the Island where the main mountain range reaches the sea. The precipitous slopes of Cronk-ny-Irey-Lhaa (nearly 1,500 feet high), the Carnanes and the Bradda Hills stretch to the Calf of Man eight miles distant. Along the whole coastline to Fleshwick there is not a single inhabited house and very few places where shore level can be reached at all on foot. This is a part of the Island that can really only be appreciated from a boat. Niarbyl formerly supported a small fleet of fishing boats manned by local farmers and crofters. The herring season ran from July to October and the proceeds were usually divided into eight shares. Three shares went to the owner of the nets, who was often a farmer, one to the owner of the boat and a share each to the four men who manned her. The introduction of new types of boats in the 1870s – the nickey and later the nobby – helped the Manx fishing industry to survive. This was at the expense of the dual occupation of farmer and fisherman, however, as fishing became almost a year-round occupation from this point. A Mrs Clague ran a cafe in Niarbyl providing refreshments at all hours of the day. She also offered full board accommodation at seven shillings per day in the bungalow on the shore, which contained four bedrooms and a sitting room.

Cregneash boasted the nearby attractions of the Chasms, Sugar-loaf Rock and caves where tea and refreshments were available from a remote cafe. This 1930s view of the village shows the Chasms Road looking towards Harry Kelly's cottage, soon to be the first element of Cregneash Village Folk Museum. The new buildings to the left belong to the Karran Farm, now the last surviving example of a traditional Manx crofting farmstead. The Karran family supplemented their income by fishing and also quarrying slate lintels from the cliff-face at Spanish Head.

THE CHASMS CAFÉ Nᵣ PORT ST MARY

The Chasms attract thousands of visitors a year to admire their spectacular views, and in the first half of the twentieth century this cafe was a very welcome sight to those who had made the journey on foot from Port Erin or Port St Mary. It was a very substantial building for such a location and remained open throughout the boom years of Manx tourism, only closing with the outbreak of war in 1939. A problem shared with the village of Cregneash was that there was no running water and the spring that supplied the cafe can still be traced in the field behind the building.

BALLAFESSON AND SURBY NEAR PORT ST MARY I.O.M.

Surby is a tiny hamlet one and a half miles north of Port Erin. This is a secluded area of narrow roads, high hedges and deep ditches and would have consisted of only about 28 houses at the time this V. L. Swales photograph was taken in the 1930s. Surby Bridge spanned a small glen known as the Luddin.

This typical Manx stiff-cart has had rails fitted to allow an extra large load to be carried. The location is Bradda and the photograph was taken by local man John Danson prior to 1914. Having been cut and left to dry in the field, the hay was later collected using carts such as this one. Expert farm workers could load a wagon with hay almost entirely from the ground, with each forkful carefully placed in sequence to bind the layer below.

Santon is the smallest parish on the Island, a narrow strip of hills and glens featuring streams and rich agricultural land. Lacking any town or large village, it is only thinly populated but offers idyllic rural scenes. The Brown Cow Inn stood a few yards north of Santon post office, on the main Douglas to Castletown road. The earliest mention of it appears in *Porter's Directory* of 1883. It provided stabling and was a popular stopping off place for the horse-drawn coaches of the day, but has been a private residence since the 1920s.

The road to Port Grenaugh is still a particularly charming one, although sadly only the concrete bases remain of the fourteen self-catering chalets that once stood down by the beach. The attractions – a shop, tea gardens and restaurant – were at the height of their popularity in 1929 when this postcard of the Harbour Road Tea Gardens was produced. The log finish to the building is reminiscent of many of the original Manx Electric Railway buildings, a style that can still be admired at Laxey station.